50 Life Lessons to

Volun

By

Alfonso Brown Jr

Table of Contents

Forward

I wrote this book because I wasn't taught these lessons as a young boy, at least not verbally, or intentionally. My father taught me many lessons by example and not instruction, and many not at all. I want my son, and all the other young boys out there, to learn these lessons early, before they make the many mistakes and bad choices I have in my life. With this book they will develop a powerful mindset and be ready for life's many challenges. I have yet to master all of these principles, as I am still a work in progress myself, which is why this book is also good for fathers and men in general. Like Lesson #11, never stop learning.

It's every Father's wish, for their son to grow up to be more and do more than they could, and I'm confident my son will have the blueprint to achieve that goal.

A mother's love and intuition is like gold, but without a father present, there will always be a void. This book is for the single mother who can do everything except think and act like a man.

I hope this book helps mold great men, because great men have the ideas, character, and drive to build great communities, which is what this world needs a lot more of, for my son and yours.

Dedication

To my son Nasir, and all the other sons of the world, may these lessons help you on your journey through life, manhood, and fatherhood.

Life Lesson Number 1:

Be Grateful

Be grateful for everything that you have. Be grateful for everything that you are and everything that you're doing. Be grateful for where you are and for the people you have around you. While it's not the best practice to compare yourself to others, when you look around the world there's a good chance that you're doing better than a lot of people. Many people would love to trade places with you, and so for this reason, I say be grateful..because it could be worse.

It could always be worse. You could be in a different situation. You could not have this and not have that, you know? And so you should constantly be in a mindset of being grateful for the opportunities that you have. Be grateful for the danger that you're not in and the negative health conditions that you don't have. Be grateful for everything.

Be grateful that when bad things happen, you were able to come out of it and found a way, or somebody helped you out, or whatever it was. Be grateful. There's always something to be grateful for. Being grateful keeps you grounded and humble and it keeps you from being greedy. It also allows you to be comfortable giving. Remember this mindset, and it will take you far in life.

Life Lesson Number 2:

Give Your Best Effort

Give your best effort simply means doing your best -but do it in everything. In everything you do, give your best. Whatever role you're playing, whatever position you have, whatever it is, you should give your best effort. That's in schoolwork, at work, as a friend, and as a son, a husband, or a brother, you give your best effort because you never know how it will pay off. You never know who is watching. You never know what blessings and opportunities may come your way. And it feels good to be the best if you are actually the best.

It also feels good to know that you gave your best, regardless of where you end up. You can relax with the outcome. Give your best effort always, in everything you do. You never know how it will pay off, and the rewards are endless.

Life Lesson Number 3:

Find Your Purpose

Find out what your purpose is on this earth. What are you supposed to be doing?

What are you supposed to be doing for a living? What are you supposed to be doing to help make the world a better place? Because that's really what it's about. We don't know exactly why we're all here and what we're supposed to do. How can you best help your family and your community in the world? What is your purpose?

People have many different purposes, and it's important to find yours because that will put you in your most comfortable state and you'll be doing what you love. You will be around people who are aligned with the things that you love, and life will be easy.

Just find your purpose, and you never know where it will take you. You also may have more than one purpose, but you have to figure it out. Explore life and gather many experiences so you can expose yourself to all life has to offer. Then you should search inside yourself to figure out what you do best and how you can best serve your family, your community, and the world.

Life Lesson Number 4:

Follow Your Passion

Follow your passion seems to be pretty self explanatory, right? Well, it is to some degree. Follow your passion, because that's what really motivates you. That's what really gets your blood pumping. That's what keeps you in a good state of mind.

Follow your passion. What do you love to do? What do you really enjoy? It doesn't mean it has to be your job, it just means your passion is something you should be doing frequently. If it's painting, rapping, singing, dancing, drawing, building, or cutting the grass. Whatever it is, if you're passionate about it, then you should seek out more opportunities to do it. Many times your passion turns into payday. I just made that up, too: *From Passion to Payday*, my new book!

Seriously, a lot of times you can get paid for doing your passion, but whether or not you do get paid with money, you will be paid with pleasure, personal pleasure, that you bring to yourself. So follow your passion. Do what you love. Don't let anybody make you forget it or put it away. Follow your passion and do what you love.

Life Lesson Number 5:

Have a Schedule

You should always have a schedule. It can be big or it can be small, but have some sort of schedule at least for the next week or, at the very least, for the next day. You should know what you're going to be doing. Whether it's nothing or it's something, you should know what you're going to be doing and where your time is going.

When you have a schedule, you can dictate what you're doing and what you don't want to do, and you won't end up doing what you don't want to do because you're going by your schedule. So, if somebody tries to interject an event or thing that you don't want to do or is just not cool or whatever, then you fall back on your schedule. "I can't do that, I'm scheduled to do [this] now." "I can't help you paint your garage, I'm scheduled to watch racing."

Protect your time. It's important to follow your schedule. First do a short-term schedule, and then make your long-term schedule. Create a schedule, follow it, and take care of it. And don't let anybody manipulate your schedule.

Life Lesson Number 6:

Go to the Top

No matter what you are doing, go to the top. At school, at work, a club, or organization, do your best and try to get to the top. There are perks at the top. There are benefits. There's pleasure. There are rewards at the top, and most people are not at the top. So it is always good to be where everyone else is not.

For example, if you are an employee, try your best to get to the top of wherever you work. Don't stay at the bottom. I worked at a job for a long time where I was at the bottom. I was down at the bottom, and moved up just a little teeny bit, but I was not focused and wired to try to get to the top. You may not like your job at the bottom. But the same place you work may be a lot better at the top or even in the middle. If you are doing your best, you may be given an opportunity to move up to a better position without even asking for it. Be the best employee you can be, and you never know what possibilities wait for you. Even if you plan on leaving your job, you want to leave at the highest position possible. Then, when you get a new job, you may not have to start at the bottom.

Doing your best at school may afford you an opportunity to apply to a special program or receive a grant or scholarship you didn't even apply for. If you are struggling with a subject, your teacher may give you extra credit because they see how hard you are working. If you try to make it to the top of the class, you could be rewarded for your efforts on the way up.

If you're in an organization, you want to go to the top because that's where the power is. That's where the decisions are made. And that's where you want to be.

The bottom line is, do your best, try to reach the top, and enjoy what happens on the way.

Life Lesson Number 7:

Take Calculated Risks

Life is going to bring many things, like opportunities or different chances to go somewhere, to get something, to be something, or to have something. Many times you may have to risk something else for what you want and where you want to go.

And it's okay to take a risk, just let it be a calculated risk, meaning that you really think it through. What are the possibilities? What are the many possible outcomes of your decision? If you do risk this or that, you may risk time and you may risk money. You may be risking a friendship. You may be risking a material possession, but take the calculated risk because you don't want to shy away from what you want or what you need. So, take a calculated risk to weigh out the options. You have to have an idea of what you stand to gain or lose in your endeavours.

Chess is a good game that is the poster child for calculated risks. You have to make moves and decide what pieces to sacrifice and look at least three moves ahead. This is a great way to make plans and decisions with your life.

Life Lesson Number 8:

Set Goals Often

Set goals every day. You should have a goal for every single day, every week, every month, and every year. You should have at least one goal for each of those time frames. Achieving goals gives you confidence. If you set small goals and you achieve them, that gives you confidence to set another goal, a bigger goal, and you just keep going.

You should always have a goal that you're trying to reach. It can be something simple, something small, or it can be something big. Have both small goals and big goals. Small goals that you probably know you can achieve, and big goals that you know are going to be really, really, really hard for you to achieve. But you should have both. They bring about discipline, because you're constantly trying to challenge yourself to see if you can reach these goals because, for the most part, we're always working against ourselves.

So if you have a goal to wake up early, just wake up trying to do that every day. If you get that out of the way, okay, cool, you did that. What's the next goal that you're trying to reach? After that, you do it again and again. Maybe you did that all week. Okay, cool. What's your weekly goal?

As you achieve the goals you set, it gives you the confidence to set bigger goals and dig deeper inside to reach new levels. Even when you fail, you will be unfazed because you have already accomplished so much. Your past successes and achieved goals will give you the fortitude to continue pursuing any goal you set for yourself. You will also be able to inspire others in their attempts at setting goals by example and by sharing the experience.

So, set goals both small and big. You'll be amazed at the person you become as you try to achieve these goals. Whether you succeed or fail, your journey could be the propeller to someone else's success.

Life Lesson Number 9:

Act Like the Person You Want to Be

You should be constantly trying to be the person you want to be. If it's someone who is confident, you should try to be confident. Act confident even though you're really not. Try to convince yourself that you are already the person you want to be or, in other words, practice being the person that you want to be.

If you're in a play or a movie, if you have a role that you're going to be playing, before you really can be good at being that character and portraying that role in the play or show, you have to practice being that person. So whether you're reading from the script or not, you are practicing trying to be that person. You want to be somebody who is kind and somebody who is good with money? Somebody who has money, somebody who is fit. You have to be working out like a fit person, you have to be trying to do the things that the person you want to be does.

This takes practice, every day. Take the time to figure out what you need to do to get closer to being the person you want to be every single day, every week, and every month. Be that person. Tell yourself that's who you are.

You could tell yourself that these are the things I have, and these are the things that I want. Because as I said before, most times we are battling ourselves, our own mind, our own being. It's you versus you. So don't tell yourself that you're weak. Tell yourself that you are strong and act strong. You may come up short sometimes, but if you keep at it, eventually you will be that strong person that you want to be.

It takes practice, it takes rehearsal. Be who you want to be right away. Start today.

Life Lesson Number 10:

The Universe Will Give You What You Ask For

Now this gets us to some deep law-of-the_universe type of philosophies, theories, and whatnot, but many people believe it's true that when you put yourself out there into the world, including what you want, what you need, and what you desire, and you focus on that, you will get it if you tell yourself who you want to be. If you keep telling yourself that, you can speak it into existence. Tell the universe what you want. Start gearing up to get the things that you need in order to be the person you want to be. The universe will start making a way for you. Start moving some stuff out the way. Start getting some stuff ready for you. I got this from a great mentor - Ash Cash - and I truly believe it. If you point yourself in a certain direction, the universe will recognize it and will help you get there. You can't give up. You can't quit. You can't sway. You have to be determined.

If you do, the universe will give you what you want. That's why some people get the good outcomes that they want and why some bad people get bad outcomes that they want. The universe doesn't care.

If a bad person wants to do something bad, often they can do it. And a lot of times, if a good person wants to do something bad, they can do it. The universe isn't the referee. It's gonna say, "You want to burn down this whole field? Okay, I mean, I don't know if that's the best thing, but hey, you are determined to do it, so I'm gonna help you do it, because here you are. If you want to plant roses and daisies in this whole field, it sounds like a beautiful idea to me. I'm gonna help you do it if you're determined to do it. If you are serious, I'll help you". So be mindful of what you want and what you ask for, because if you move in the right way you will get it whether it's good or bad. So choose wisely.

Life Lesson Number: 11

Never Stop Learning

We start learning right away, as a baby. You don't know exactly what you're learning, but you're learning everything that you can. As a baby, you're learning everything every day, every minute. As you get older you stop learning as much on a daily basis, but depending on what your life is like, you may work in an industry where you just learn a lot every day. A lot of information comes your way, you talk to a lot of people, you learn information. But some people don't work or naturally exist in an environment where they are constantly learning things every day. That doesn't mean that you can't still learn something every day.

Books and libraries can help with that and so can the internet and smartphones. You can learn something every day. You can learn a new language. You can learn new information about new industries or technology, or you can learn about history. You can learn new techniques, new recipes, new strategies, and new moves. You can learn many things. There's no cap, there's no max, on what you can learn and how much you can learn.

So take advantage of that, and learn as much as possible. Use what you've learned to better yourself, your community, and the world beyond

Life Lesson Number 12:

Take Your Health Seriously

Our health is really our number-one asset. I mean besides time, we can debate health or time, but you can have a lot of time and bad health. It's just a waste. We don't know how much time we have on this earth, and you do need to take care of your time, but you absolutely need to take your health seriously. You can have a lot of money, but if you're unhealthy, you can't enjoy it.

Watch what you eat. Make sure you exercise. Don't put any foreign substances in your body, no matter who else has done it and survived or is doing just fine. Everyone's body is different. Take your health seriously. Be grateful for good health and try your best to maintain it. Once your health is going bad, your number-one priority is trying to get back to good health. It's like you can't do anything else. You can barely work if you don't already have some kind of passive income set up or somebody just taking care of you. You will need to work, and it's hard to work in bad health. You can easily find programs and systems to follow and guide you. Or you can ask a mentor or someone you believe to be healthy. Take your health seriously, and be grateful for good health.

Life Lesson Number 13:

Always Have a Plan

You should always have a plan, some sort of plan, of what you're going to do. It might not be a good plan, but at least you have a plan. If you have a plan, you may run into some information that changes that bad plan into a good plan but having a plan gives you some direction and focus. It ensures that you're just not in a freefall. Have a plan for everything. Have a plan for your day, kind of like your schedule. Know what you are going to do.

Have a plan for your life, or your schooling and your career. Have a plan for your relationship. Have a plan for your family. You should always have a plan, because it will guide you and many times it will protect you. It can guide you to the right place and people while keeping you from going to the wrong place with the wrong people.

A plan gives you confidence. You have worked out the ins and outs, calculated the risks and potential results, so you feel good. People around you are at ease and comfortable when they know you have a plan. Once again, others will respect you for having thought out a plan, and you will respect yourself.

It can also be a good practice to have a contingency plan. Just in case. Your original plan may not work. However, your second plan could be correct. Like I said, plans don't always work, so be prepared.

Life Lesson Number 14:

Be Prepared

Just be prepared. Be prepared for everything and anything that you can be prepared for. If you're going to school, you should have things you need for school in your backpack and in your locker.

Do you have a car? You should be prepared for the car to break down. So you need insurance and you definitely need money. Life insurance … be prepared because, so far, throughout history, death is guaranteed. Death is undefeated. So that's an easy one, but there are many times when we can be prepared both for little things and big things.

You know, it's very easy, like having a jacket when it might be cold.

You are prepared. Have some gloves if you're doing some work. You might have a pop quiz or a pop test. You should be studying every night.

Be prepared for what life may throw at you. Many times we have hints and clues from previous experiences or other people's experiences so we can be prepared for a lot in life. It's just much better to try and prepare for bad things and for good things. Preparation will definitely help make your life easier.

Life Lesson Number 15:

Don't Give Up

It may look like you're not gonna make it. There have been times that it looked like I just wasn't gonna make it. But I didn't give up. I just kept going.

You might be running late for a flight, but you get to the airport and there's nobody in line. You may get some people in line, but you're able to skip the line. Maybe the flight is delayed, you never know. But you can't give up. You have got to keep trying.

I know this because I've done it, and I've been successful.

Even if sometimes you don't believe that you will make it and achieve what you're trying to accomplish, you still don't give up. You keep going.

So you may think, *This is never going to work*, but if you keep going, if you still keep trying, you may be surprised.

Many times you will be surprised. If you have a big goal of becoming something or creating something or building something, you have to keep going. Even when you're met with adversity or disaster and twists and turns, ups and downs, Don't Give Up.

If it's something you say you want, something you truly need, Don't Give Up. You keep going until there is 100 percent evidence that you can't do it or have it. Even then, maybe you just modify your goal or accomplishment to get what you want. Just do your best, try your best, and go the distance.

Life Lesson Number 16:

99 Percent of Your Problems Are Your Fault

This is a lesson you should try to understand quickly. It's also an important perspective to adopt as well. Good things and bad things will happen in your life, and you will give credit or place blame in every situation. However, when you look closely, you will see that 99 percent of the time, you are responsible.

When you get good grades in school or a promotion at work, do they just like you or randomly pick you to reward? Or did you actually earn and deserve what you got? When you fail or get fired, were they hating on you or did your performance dictate the outcome?

Whether you're late or early, in a good relationship or bad, what was your role in the process? Everything that happens to you can usually be traced back to a decision or choice you made. That 1 percent is just unpredictable people or weather or some uncontrollable event—good or bad.

Be mindful of the choices and decisions you make, because they can dictate your fate in the future, either near or far.

Life Lesson Number 17:

Always Have Protection

Now this one is serious. It's lighthearted, but it's very serious. Always have protection. Notice this protection is primarily in relation to women and being with women intimately. You should always have it because you know what your goal is, you know what you want to do, and you're just not that strong. As a man, you really may not be that strong. Most men aren't that strong or aren't that disciplined in those moments, and if you don't have protection you may go without, especially if you get permission. So always have it because you don't want to end up in a position or with responsibilities that you did not intend to have.

In other areas of your life, I'm speaking of insurance. Always get insurance.

I mean, you know, for the most part, for big items, big situations, rental cars, you know, high-ticket items, you get the insurance. You should be buying whatever it is with enough money left over to be able to afford the insurance. That's protecting yourself from an unwanted outcome.

Life insurance is protection. Knowing how to physically defend yourself is protection. Now whether or not you have an actual weapon, you know, that's something you can consider as well.

Whether you're carrying a weapon or whether you've learned and trained your hands and your body to be a weapon, that is protection. You should always have it, because you never know where and when you'll need it. In case somebody tries something on you and you're prepared to protect yourself and the people you care about.

So always have protection, wherever you think you may need it or not.

Life Lesson Number 18:

Always Speak Your Mind

As a man, as a human being of masculine energy, a strong figure, a warrior, a god, you should always speak your mind and not be afraid to say what you have to say.

You should never be afraid to express your feelings.

Now obviously there are exceptions dealing with certain occasions and certain people, like maybe your mom, or you know you're in a certain venue or setting where it's better to hold your full opinion back for the greater good of the situation. You'll have to learn to assess this. But in general, you should speak your mind and not bite your tongue. It feels better when you speak your mind. People respect you more when you're truthful. They may not always like your position, but they will respect that you said what you had to say and didn't hold back, and didn't wait until later. You didn't water it down. You tell people how you feel about a certain situation, and it's up to them to deal with it. Now you can't change how you feel, so you might as well say it.

Hey, this is what I think ... Now there is a way to be proper, maybe delicate, with how you say what you have to say. You know when dealing with certain situations, of course, you don't have to be so hard all the time and give your opinion with malice and bad intent. If you don't like something you don't like it, but you don't have to make someone else feel bad about you not liking whatever they have or whatever they did. However, your opinion is your opinion, and you should stick to it. You shouldn't hide it, and there is a way that you can do this.

Many times people come to me with music. They say, "Hey man I made a song, check out my song." Then I listened to the song and it was straight whack, it was trash, but I didn't tell him it was trash. I didn't say "Hey, yo man, that's wack!" That's unnecessary.

What I did say was, "Hey, I'm really not feeling it, it's not my taste. You don't have to go full throttle all the time, especially with people that you don't know. You do have to give your honest opinion. Even with food, a lot of times people pretend that they like someone else's cooking. If you don't like it, you don't like it. If you say you like it, you may get it again. Now you gotta eat that nasty food twice!

So always speak your mind with men and with women with everybody. You respect yourself and others will respect you too.

Life Lesson Number 19:

Control your emotions

This lesson is very important because you'll find that when you do control your emotions in every situation, you end up with a better result. Whether dealing with work, family, or sports, you need to control your emotions. That's what a man does. Men are not overly emotional. Men think, we're calm, and we calculate. Women are emotional. Now that's not to say that a man does not have emotions because we do, you just have to control them. You have to take a deep breath, take a step back, calm yourself down and think. Use your head, and not your heart, because your emotions come from your heart. Good decisions and choices, they both come from your mind. Women will try to get you in your emotions. If you care for a woman, you will be dealing with your emotions more than your mind. And that's why women are dangerous. No, seriously, but that's why you have to be careful with women.

Take your time, because they'll have you wallowing in your emotions when you need to use your brain. So, control your emotions because it can save you from doing damage to yourself, your career, or your life. It Really just depends. So be a man and control your emotions.

Life Lesson Number 20: Don't Waste Time

Time is so, so, so important. It's so valuable. As you know, we do not know how much time we have left. Like everybody, we think we have a lot of time. But as proven through the lives of others, we really don't know when our time is up.

Now that's on a macro level, just of life in general. Don't waste your time here on this earth. But on a micro level, when you have things to do, you have business to handle, tasks to complete, and needs to be met, you don't want to waste time then, either. You want to identify where you can best use your time and identify ways to not waste time. Most importantly, don't let anybody else waste your time because people will do it.

You will fall into the trap of letting somebody else waste your time doing something that you don't want to do.

You will look back and say, "I wasted all this time and I didn't even want to do this." So use your time wisely. It is the most valuable thing you have. Well, other than your health. Protect your time.

I say protect it from other people. You can get help with your time from apps on your phone. You know, that's why in a previous chapter we say get a schedule. Have a schedule. Have a plan. These are things that help you manage your time well. Knowing what you have coming up will save you from wasting time and being lost and being stuck. The more you use your time wisely, the more you can use your time leisurely. You have work to do, you get up and get it done.

Knock it out. If you have errands to run, you go run them. Don't waste time.

Cut people off if you need to. "Hey, I gotta call you back." "Hey, I gotta go."

Turn the TV off and go do what you have to do. Then you'll see that you have more time for yourself to do the things that you really love doing.

Be extremely protective of your time. Don't waste it, and don't let others waste it for you.

Life Lesson Number 21:

Enjoy Every Day

Every day is a gift, that's why they call it the present. I don't know who said it, but it's good and it makes sense.

The point is, every day that you're here, every day that you're alive, you have an opportunity to smile and laugh and have fun. You should do it. You may have work to do or business to handle, or you may receive bad news or something, but if you can, take a step back and realize that this day is a gift and take at least a portion of it and just enjoy it. Whether you just enjoy the way the sky looks, talk to somebody that makes you laugh, watch something, or do something that brings you pleasure and joy. It could be for as little as thirty minutes. Your whole day doesn't have to be working or sorrow.

You have twenty-four hours, so you can take some time to just enjoy your day, enjoy life, and then you can get back to whatever is more pressing in your life. Be mindful of just the blessing of having a day to be alive.

Life Lesson Number 22:

Perspective Is Everything

Perspective is the way that you see a certain situation. Many situations have many different perspectives. You see something one way, another person may see it a different way. If you have something happen to you, you can see it as bad or you can see it as good.

Your perspective is what dictates your reality. You can think it is really hot outside or you can think that it's too hot outside, or you can say "Wow, it's nice and hot outside. I'm going to get in the pool."

Take the letter W, for example. If you turn it once, it can be an E. Turn it again and it's an "M", turn it once more and you have a 3. Same letter, but four different people could see something different, depending on their perspective.

If your movie gets cancelled, you can say "Man, I'm mad my movie was cancelled." or "man, my movie was cancelled, now I can handle this business. Now I can go do this other thing." Your perspective is everything. It will govern your choices and decisions, and it'll be your barometer for how you feel.

It's okay to change your perspective. You may look at a situation or issue one way on Monday and then on Tuesday, maybe you feel a different way. Maybe you've got a new perspective, whether you came up with it on your own or you heard someone else's perspective and now you agree with that more. It's perfectly fine. Perspective is important, though, it's important to take the time to look at certain things and situations from different angles from a different Perspective. That way, you know if you're looking at it the right way for the situation. So be smart and be mindful that your perspective is everything.

Life Lesson Number 23:

Take Advantage of Every Opportunity

In this life, there are not always many opportunities sent your way. They depend on the things you do, your environment, and your situation. Opportunities depend on many factors.

You may have a lot of opportunities, you may have a few opportunities, but you should take advantage of every one. Don't let an opportunity pass for you to better yourself, improve your position, or to reach a goal or achievement. There could be an opportunity to gain knowledge or experience, or maybe just to meet someone who could help you out in the future. You could be given the chance to display your skills or talents, which could be just what you need, but if you decline or miss that opportunity you could regret it.

Life Lesson Number 24:

Be Well Rounded and Versatile

It's important to gain knowledge and experience in many different fields and avenues of life. The world has so much to offer and there are so many opportunities that can be available to you if you are well rounded, if you're able to move in a certain way in many different situations, and if you're able to hold many different conversations.

When you're well rounded, it means that you can play a little basketball, maybe a little football, and some tennis. You can play checkers, maybe some chess. You can eat at a Japanese or Indian restaurant. You want to be well rounded and versatile because you open up more doors of life, leading to more fun, more pleasure, more access, and more opportunity.

If you're looking to get into a certain position, whether it's a job or a certain club you're going to, it will benefit you to be well rounded and versatile. If you're one dimensional and you're not much of an asset then you're not that intriguing as a person, but when you can move in different rooms and wear different shoes you add more value to yourself. More value brings more life, so open yourself up to the world.

Life Lesson Number 25:

Always Invest

You should always be investing, whether in yourself or in other opportunities. Always be on the lookout for a way to invest in yourself.

Investments like this include a course or class, some sort of training that can improve your skills or knowledge or can just make you a better person. Invest in other opportunities that can bring you more money. More money brings more time. More time brings more freedom. Freedom brings more pleasure and happiness, so always invest. Invest in companies, invest in people, and, most importantly, investing yourself.

The returns may not be immediate, but they will build up over time. You look up and suddenly you are a major asset and you may own some valuable, smaller assets, all because you're constantly looking to invest. Some good ways to invest are stocks, real estate, startup companies, and personal courses.

Life Lesson Number 26:

Learn to Make Decisions Quickly

This is an important lesson, because you can miss opportunities. If you take too long when making decisions, you can put yourself in a bad position. You can make the wrong decision by taking too long and thinking too much. Many times when we have a decision to make, our first instinct is usually the correct one. There have been plenty of times where you may have a decision to make and you already have the answer but you think about it, calculate, contemplate, then at the end, you come back to that first thought.

Making decisions quickly helps build confidence as well because, as stated, nine times out of ten it is making the right decision in the rain whether it was a bad outcome or not. It still may be the right decision versus the absolute wrong decision, but you don't want to waste time. So you want to learn and train your mind to assess the situation or issue and pump out a decision quickly.

Life Lesson Number 27:

Life Insurance

Life insurance is one of the top ways to ensure that your family will have an inheritance, something that you leave them. Suppose that your father left you and somebody else you know a lot of money or just enough money to take care of some important situations. Life insurance is a very good thing to have. It is a responsible tool or asset to have in place.

Obviously, you need to learn to do the research about whether to get a term-life or whole-life policy. Figure out which one is better for you and your family. Life Insurance is definitely something that everybody should have, every man should have. That way he's taken care of, because you always want to take care of yourself. So whether that's being able to pay for your funeral arrangements, or if you have a family that you leave behind, then you want to be able to take care of those things. So, life insurance is very important. You must get it.

Life Lesson Number 28:

Buy a Multifamily Property as Your First Home

This could be up for debate for some people, but it's a very good practice. It's been proven that it's a very good practice to make this type of purchase as your first home, you know, while your credit is still good or whatever, while you're still young enough that you can still tolerate that kind of living situation, depending on how it is.

So, buy a property that's a duplex or more, maybe three or four units. You live in one unit and you can rent out the other units to other people. Those tenants, when they pay the rent, that money, that income will pay for your mortgage as well. And you'll be living for free. There are plenty of people online and real estate professionals, real estate investors that promote this type of purchase, because it has proven to be very beneficial and a good beginning for wealth building. So it's definitely something to look into. Get the multifamily property, your first one, while you're young, and work your way up to your own private residence.

Life Lesson Number 29:

Start Buying Christmas Gifts Early

Start buying your Christmas gifts in October or earlier.. Now, obviously this one you know isn't just some supreme level of wisdom or whatever, and that you need to have something you need to do and this will make your life so much better. It is a good practice though, and it will come in handy. If you have any ideas of what to get, write your list. It's all about being prepared, having preparation and whatnot, and just being early so you put together a little list of who should get a gift from you. And you start by knocking them off one by one. You may not have a lot of money, but you want to get people gifts, like your family, perhaps your significant other. If you have kids, start early, just grabbing this and that here and there. By the time December comes around, you already have your shopping taken care of and you're ready to go. Then, when the holiday sales do come out, everybody is done and you are just shopping for yourself for low, low prices. Try it, because last minute shopping can be overwhelming.

Life Lesson Number 30:

Diversify Your Wardrobe

It's always good to have a well-rounded wardrobe. You want to be comfortable in different environments, different arenas, you don't want to just be an urban gear streetwear guy and you don't want to always just be in casual clothes, or a button up. You want to be able to mix it up. Start early, and get used to wearing different types of clothing. See how you look and find your style, and you will always be comfortable. So when it's time, you can just throw on a suit that you know looks really good for work or for special occasions. You already have it in your closet, so you know what you're going to wear and you don't have to be looking around and asking for advice.

You can have expert advice, but you don't have to be trying to decide what to wear at the last minute when it's time to do something. You want to get that locked down early and as a part of your normal wardrobe. Just come out on a Tuesday with a suit on, everybody's gonna ask you where are you going? You can just say, "anywhere." So, the next day, you got your fly urban wear. Or maybe you're just really laid-back, low key, but it's good to have a variety of clothing in your wardrobe. That way you feel and look comfortable in different environments that you may find yourself in. People respect someone who can dress well for different occasions. So, it's very good practice to having an extensive wardrobe and be able to move in different environments.

Life Lesson Number 31:

Learn How to Cook

Learn how to cook three meals a day. Learn how to cook what you like for breakfast, lunch, and dinner. Whatever your favourite meals are, figure out how to make them, that way you don't have to be held hostage by other people who know how to make the stuff that you like. They may make it better but at least you know how.

Keep practicing at it until you get good and until somebody likes yours more than they like their own. This way if you're on your own, you will be able to eat well and not have to eat out. You have the capacity to learn all kinds of technical and complex mechanisms, equations, and situations. You can learn how to cook, it just takes a little time, a little practice, and a little bit of basic knowledge and you'll be doing it right. You might even start liking it. We all like good food. So, definitely make time to learn, watch how somebody does it, that makes the food you like, or get somebody to teach you, but learn to be able to feed yourself food that is good.

Life Lesson Number 32:

Skills Pay Bills, so Learn at Least Two

You can support yourself if you have certain skills. There are plenty of common skills and there are plenty of unique skills that are needed in the world, and to our society and our people. People who have those skills are paid good money. If you always have that skill, and you nurture it, master it, you will always be able to take care of yourself.

Make sure you pick a skill that is definitely needed in multiple environments and applications, and you will do well in life and your career. Find something you'd like to do and learn more than one skill, that way you can switch if you get bored with a particular career. There are many different ways that you can go about using those skills, whether you work for a firm or company or working for yourself. You want to have the skills that are necessary, the skills that maybe your family needs, and you can help them.

You don't have to limit it to two, but learn as many skills as you can learn and you will see how far they take you, how many doors they open for you, how many opportunities they bring your way, and soon you will be able to provide for yourself and your family.

This is very important. Learn a skill, learn three skills. Learn as many as you can, and you'll go far.

Life Lesson Number 33:

Never Sit with Your Back to the Door

While we don't live in, a movie or whatnot, where you're a spy and it's dangerous, or you just live in some gangster society or whatever. But it's a good practice to, if possible, not sit with your back to the door. That way you can be ready. It's all about being ready and prepared should that door bust open with somebody with ill intentions.

There will be a couple of seconds where you see what's going on and you can make a move to save yourself or save people you care about. If all goes well, you may not ever need this wisdom, and it may not ever arise where it was good that you did not have your back to the door, but it's still a good practice. Women like it, too, that you know not to have you back to the door because they feel like you could protect and you are aware of your surroundings. You never know, but it's just a good practice. So don't sit with your back to the door or the window. You want to be ready to see what's coming at you.

Life Lesson Number 34:

Put Your Cash in Your Pocket, Not Your Wallet

Now this is a little tip that I've been using for a long time. I'm not sure where I got it, but I found it to make sense. Because you hear about people losing their wallet. "I lost my wallet," "Get my wallet," "Where's my wallet?" "Somebody stole my wallet." If you have your cards, your ID, and your cash in your wallet and you do lose it, then they are all gone, versus if you've got your cards and your ID in your wallet. If you have cash money in your pocket you may lose money, which is rare, but if you lose your wallet, you still have that cash.

Granted, you may not have a lot of cash, and that might be another lesson: Make sure you have enough cash for basic daily needs. But if you keep your cash loose in your pocket, that way you won't be left with nothing in the event that you leave your wallet or it somehow falls out.

It's just a good idea not to have all of your money in one place on your body. You may get robbed, you may leave your wallet on a counter, but you still have $100 in your pocket. Now you can get home.

Life Lesson Number 35:

Keep a Journal to Write Down Ideas

It is very important to write down your thoughts, your goals, your aspirations, your passions. If you put it down on paper or have a little book where you can have these ideas that come to you, there's a good chance you will achieve them. God sends you ideas that he wants you to carry out, that he wants you to bring to life, and you need to have a record of things you'd like to do, and things you come up with. Write them down. That way they're ready when the time comes.

If an opportunity comes, you can go and say "Yeah, that's right. I wanted to do this and now I have the chance or, you just got your thoughts articulated, and now you don't want to forget something. You may think of a cool idea, a revolutionary idea, and if you don't write it down because of life and whatever else is going on, you forget it. Maybe you never remember it or you remember it late and somebody else has already done your idea.

Or maybe that energy was out there in the universe of somebody's family, and you didn't have it ready and written down, so you never got around to it. You never started it, and it either never came out or somebody else brought it up. So it's definitely a good practice to have a journal to write down your thoughts, feelings, and ideas. That way, you don't forget them. Maybe even years later, your son, your daughter, or somebody else reads your journal, sees your idea, and brings it to life. Then you've done your job, even if you're not here.

Life Lesson Number 36:

Women Respect Money, Power, and Honesty

This is what gets them going. This is what they like. I mean, they're all pretty. Really. They like money, women like money. Women are drawn to power. And women respect you when you're honest. Women like to have money. They like to spend money.

They like a man to have money. Women don't want to have to get money. They want to have money. They want to have you know that they're wired to want to take care of the person with money. That's how women are, you know men are wired to get money. And all money is protection. Safety, comfort. Resources are important to women. But, so is security to many.

Everybody needs security, and women especially need it, so you should definitely focus on money. Just plain and simple. Women love power. Power means that they can get certain things done that they need done. Power is protection as well. Women crave security, they crave it, they need it. Power is attractive, power is needed to get certain things done. Some things don't require a lot of power, but there are other things in life that do require power, and if you have it, you will be desired.

Women also love honesty. They may not love the honest words that come out of your mouth, however.

I mean, I love the honest actions that are portrayed, but women respect honesty and respect is the most important thing you want from a woman, so always be honest. Be 99.9 percent honest, it's always that 1 percent that you just can't tell them. You just can't. But 99 percent of the time, you need to just be honest. Let them have it. If they don't like it, they need to go because this is what they want from you: Honesty. Also it feels better when you're honest. So tell the truth.

Life Lesson Number 37:

Never Chase a Woman

This is a straightforward statement that really doesn't need a whole lot of words and talking behind it. For the sake of you know the people that need a little extra, never chase a woman. She should be chasing you, as she's already got a couple of other people chasing her already.

You don't want to be one of those guys. You want to stand out, and even if you do want this one, don't chase her. You should be chasing yourself, chasing the best version of yourself. She's going to see this version and now she's going to be chasing you. Just try it, don't chase at all.

Life Lesson Number 38:

You May Need to Care for Your Parents as They Age

Life is about cycles. You progress from a baby to a toddler, then a child and a teenager, and then a young adult, and then an adult, and then you'll be an adult for a while. And people were taking care of you most of that time, and then you take care of yourself, and then you stop being able to take care of yourself, depending on the circumstances. So, depending on the decisions and actions and outcomes that your parents have with their lives, they can either take care of themselves financially and physically or they can't and they need help. The primary person who is going to be responsible is you. You are going to have to help take care of the people who have cared for you the most and who love you the most and who need you now, simply because they can't take care of themselves.

Sometimes it starts out small, helping them here and there with this and that, money or just physical things like moving stuff or running errands. Whatever it is, it may start off small, and then it may get more consistent, more frequent, to where you need to really, you know, give them a lot of money and really help them do more things because they know they can, there is less that they can do physically when it comes to driving and handling their business and whatnot. You will have to be able to help out as much as you can and it will be wonderful if you could really do a great job at it.

If it's money and being able to have a good amount to really be able to take care of them without it being a strain on you and your family.

Obviously, if you have money, you usually have a considerable amount of free time, and with that time, you can help them do the things they need to do. So just be mindful that the tables will turn and some of your parents may be able to do everything they need all the way up until the end. However, there is a chance that they may need a lot more of your help as they get older, both financially and physically.

Life Lesson Number 39:

Don't Be Afraid to Say No

No is one of the best words in the English language.

No is a powerful word. It is a liberating word. It is a fearless word. It's a good word. Throughout your life, people will ask you for things, to do stuff, to give them things, to say things, to go places … actually, all kinds of stuff and, depending on that person, you may feel compelled to say yes, based on whatever their circumstances are. But their circumstances don't matter. Yours do. If someone asks you to do something you really don't want to do, regardless of how much they need it, you can say no.

If Someone needs you to do something or be somewhere or be somebody that you don't want to be, you can say "No." It's okay. No is actually a really good thing. People really don't care about what other people need and what they have going on. People care about themselves. People have emergencies that come up in their lives. An emergency can range from "I forgot my phone at home" to "Oh, my god, I forgot I have to pick up my child." "Can you take me home to get my phone?" That's an emergency to them, but not to you. You may have something better to do. You should have something better to do.

Saying no and being okay with it is what you have to work on, because people will try to make you feel bad. Your own brain may, even your heart may try to make you feel bad. You can't be soft, put yourself first and say no when you want.

Life Lesson Number 40:

Doing Something a Little Bit at a Time Is Better than Doing Nothing at All

This principle has many applications. You may say, "I need to save money, every week, every month, but you're just saving, one dollar, five dollars, or ten dollars. It adds up though. You can do something small, but be consistent with it. If you keep doing it, it will add up. If you practice something little by little, that practice will add up. If you work out little by little, that working out will add up. It will build up. You'll see results.

Doing nothing at all, however, because you feel like you're not doing enough means you will end up with nothing. It's really quite simple. But this one is a battle with your mind, because your mind says "I need to do more. If I can't do hours worth, it's not good enough. I can't save $100, that's not enough.

Be smarter, because if you don't do anything, you won't get anything. You won't have anything, but if you do it little by little over time, you will have something and you can always increase what you're doing. You can fluctuate from month to month or from week to week. One week you can go up and be doing a lot. The next month you're gonna come down and be doing a little bit more, as you keep going. Don't stop, and you will reach your end result.

Life Lesson Number 41:

Give Your Stomach and Body a Rest

Growing up, they always said you need three meals a day, breakfast, lunch, and dinner. Times have changed, information has come out, and so have new theories and philosophies and perspectives. The bottom line is that you do need to keep yourself hydrated and keep yourself healthy with proper nourishment.

You do not have to give yourself a big meal three times per day. You can mix it up, and you can do what your body feels. It could be a light breakfast. It could be no lunch, and it could be a big dinner. It could be a big dinner and next day no breakfast and no lunch. It's not like you're going to starve or that you have to eat because you ate last night. What you're doing is letting your stomach recover. Everyone can go at least 48hrs without eating.

Maybe your stomach doesn't process food as fast as others do. Even if it processes quickly, you still want it to just be able to have the time that it needs. It's perfectly okay to take a meal off. You can eat something small if you want, but you don't have to constantly eat meal after meal after meal because you think that's what your body needs, because it doesn't.

Your body does need rest. When your body needs rest, it's important to try to point out the times throughout your day and week when you can get some rest because there's nothing going on. You don't have things to do. There's nobody around you at that time, so go ahead and rest up.

Maybe you're resting up because you have a busy week coming up or maybe you just had a busy week. And you should use that opportunity to give your body the rest that it needs and that it wants. There's no need to overdo it, you know what your body is telling you. You don't want your body to force you to get some rest, because it might come at the wrong time. You may oversleep and miss a deadline because you were so tired you didn't hear your alarm clock. Then you get sick. So give your body what it needs. That's nourishment, nutrients, and time to rest and recoup.

Life Lesson Number 42:

Check and Double-Check Everything

It's a very good practice to check what you're doing at school and at work. If you have the chance, check things to make sure that you got it right and actually look good. Use this if you think you need to double check. Do it, maybe on something as simple as getting ready to go to a restaurant to pick up food. You could just call and check to make sure they're open. Maybe they should be open, but for whatever reason they aren't. Maybe they're usually not open on Mondays and you forgot or maybe they look closed, but you'll save yourself some time and some energy.

If you just make the easy call and check if you've got to be somewhere for yourself or somebody else and you think it's at 7 a.m. It wouldn't hurt to just check. Check the paperwork, make sure it really was 7 a.m. You could call somebody or call the place you go to, just to ask "Hey, I just want to double check and make sure that this starts at 7am."

You very seldom lose if you check and double check. When you're taking a test if you have time, check, if you have more time, double check. When you type in a text message or especially the Internet, because you know the internet is undefeated make sure you check and double check. You don't want to look dumb or stupid for writing misspelled words, and just stuff that don't make sense for the whole world to see.

You don't want to assume something costs one price that you can't afford without checking because you could actually have the money. There are so many reasons to check and double check which will save you time, money, and opportunity. So use this in every facet of life that you see fit and I doubt you'll go wrong.

Life Lesson Number 43:

Find a Way to Execute on Your Dream

This one is really kind of simple, and maybe I'll just keep it really simple. If you have a dream, something that you really want to do, something you're really passionate about for whatever the reason, find a way to get it done. Find a way to achieve that dream. Ask anybody what to do, where to get help. Try any avenue and any method. Look high, look low, and anywhere in between.

Find a way to get it done. Ask questions, check and double check, leave no stone unturned. If it's your dream and you really want to bring it to fruition, then you need to do whatever you need to do using whatever is at your disposal to bring it to life.

That's it. If you have a dream, go for it. Don't stop, go for it. If you are met with hurdles, roadblocks, and dead ends you just find a way you keep going and find a way to succeed.

Life Lesson Number 44:

Keep your room, house, and car Clean and Neat

This is very simple as well. It's super simple. Keep your stuff clean. Do it for yourself, so that your stuff is clean. Do for yourself, so that your stuff is neat and organized and so that when you need something you can readily go and get it. You can use it and, of course, externally it looks good to everyone else if your stuff is clean, and neat, and if it's intact, if it's organized. You will look like someone who is trustworthy and reliable and responsible.

People will also respect you from how you look. If it's neat, work on getting into the habit of starting early. We all know the easiest way to make your bed in the morning: Get out of bed and make it right away. That's a win. Do that, and then you just do a daily activity, a daily mantra of *I'm gonna keep my stuff neat.* Make sure it's clean. Make sure it's organized. That will take you a long way. It'll save you time. It'll save you energy and it may even open doors for you. It may even present you with opportunities. You never know where opportunities come from, so do yourself a favour and keep your life clean, neat, and organized.

Life Lesson Number 45:

Book Your Reservations Early Whenever Possible

If you know you have an event or an outing or a need for a reservation coming up, book it early if you can, plain and simple. If you know you're going to a restaurant, go ahead and book the reservation as early as you can. If you need to book a flight, go ahead and take care of it if you have the money to do it. Go ahead and book the flight, rental car, hotel room. Reserve movie tickets. It just makes life so much easier when you reserve your activities early and in advance. Now, if you don't have the time you don't have the time. Obviously if the decision was made at the last minute it's the last minute. But when you do know about something, if you can book it early, just book it. You can always cancel and you can always modify.

This makes your life easy, because when those events and activities come up, you're already ready. You already have priority selection when you reserve, so you know you're not picking from the last bit available. Now you don't have to change your plans. Also, this looks good to people from outside. They'll say "Wow, this guy is really on point. He had the reservation ready." Those types of actions can also lead to opportunities and you always want to be doing things that create opportunities for yourself.

First and foremost, this is for the quality of your life, to reduce stress. It is very stressful when you have to book a reservation at the last minute and now what you want is not available or maybe you have to pay more than you want to pay. It's just not a good look. So do yourself a favour and reserve and book as early as possible.

Life Lesson Number 46:

Do Not Neglect Your Hobbies

Throughout life, you probably grew up liking to do certain things, or you gained new activities that you like to do and whatnot. But because of work or family, many times we get sidetracked or we let those hobbies fall to the wayside as we're tending to other matters. Those matters are arguably more important, but not way more important. Your hobbies or the things that you like to do are things that make you happy. Also, items that you collect. You know things you want to have that make you feel good. Keep pursuing those things consistently. You want to make time for it in your life, which is why having a schedule is so important. You have a busy schedule, which you know works in your family. That's cool, but find a way to fit in what you like to do. Just be you. It will help with your peace. Everybody else isn't really worried about your time and what you have going on.

Like I said before, people care about themselves. And people may or may not notice that you don't do the things you like to do. You don't go to places you'd like to go. You don't have the things you'd like to have because you put all these other things before it. So do yourself a favour and keep your hobbies that you enjoy. Keep those things at the forefront of your life. Don't forget about them. If you forget about them, you forget about you. And you have to take care of YOU.

It doesn't have to be the same proportion of time as everything else, but it does need to be a part of your life, so get your planner and your schedule and make sure that you do the things that you'd like to do. Take care of you.

Life Lesson Number 47:

Understand Your Strengths and Weaknesses

It's important to take a look at yourself, right? Analyse yourself and learn about yourself. This one is especially important because it will help you along the way. If you understand your strengths, then you know what you can do. If you know what you're good at, you know what tasks of your life you need to do yourself. When you know your weaknesses, you know the things you shouldn't be doing. The things that you need to get help with, and ask somebody else to do for you.

So whether you're just running your regular life or things that you can take care of in your life because you're good at that. If it's a strength, then that's what you should be doing. But if it's parts of your life that you're weak in , you need to get help. You need to get somebody else to handle it. At least until maybe you turn a weakness into a strength, because that is a possibility. You know, just because something is a weakness now doesn't mean it has to stay a weakness. You can learn or you can work at your weakness, and actually turn it into a strength.

That's one thing to be mindful of, and to explore. Are there any weaknesses that I can turn into strengths? You understand your strengths and your weaknesses. If it's something that you're strong at, you should be doing it in your business and your relationship, and something that there's a weak area then you should have an employee or spouse handle. It's just easier, it relieves stress and it comands respect because it shows that you don't have an ego. You know, once again, this is something that you're always looking for, but this is something that people respect. You know and respect somebody who can say, "Hey, I'm not good at this. Can you help me? Or hey, I think you're better at doing this."Would you do this please? You're still gonna benefit from it so it won't hurt you. This is just another lesson that you should definitely learn from.

So pay attention to yourself, and try to turn some weaknesses into strengths.

Life Lesson Number 48:

Being Alone Is Therapeutic and Healthy

Being alone is really a blast. I mean when you really embrace being alone, it is really a wonderful thing. You're doing what you want when you want. Eat what you want and watch what you want. Listen to what you want, and know you don't have to share, since it's, you know, quiet. Do not underestimate the power of being alone for any period of time, especially if you use that alone time wisely. This means that you know how to use that time to think about your life or your past and future.

Think about ways to improve your life. Use that time to work out and exercise. Get your body in shape. Get your business in order, get your closet clean. Being alone has many benefits, including that it is extremely peaceful and calming. When you're the only voice that you hear, it is comforting knowing that if you need to, you can reach out and hear somebody else's voice and get some company, hang out, then you can do that. You can pop away from your aloneness like Bruce Wayne, and go out, meet some people, have fun, and then you can come back and be by yourself. You can meditate, or you can just relax. You have your positive energy, uninterrupted by anyone else when you're alone.

If you have the opportunity, because it's all about perspective, right. So, being alone is an opportunity. And if you get that opportunity, you should embrace it and use it to your benefit. It is a plus not a minus, and you're in control of how long you're alone. It's just that simple. So be mindful, and don't be afraid to be alone.

Life Lesson Number 49:

Find a Mentor in Areas Where you Need Help

Many successful people will tell you that a mentor can help you improve certain parts of your life. Part of the reason they reach that success is that they had a mentor, whether they are just successful in life or successful in business, they will tell you that they had a mentor. Some people may have more than one mentor. You can have a different mentor for different areas of your life.

If you're running different businesses, you may need a mentor for each one. You may need a mentor to help you learn how to cook, for example. A mentor is some sort of teacher, some sort of person, who knows more than you, who has proven themselves, and is doing the things you want to do.

This person can be anybody from anywhere, if you feel like they are someone who is qualified to give you guidance and instruction on how to go about a certain task, procedure, or endeavor that you are getting into. Then you request this person's time, energy, and knowledge in helping you achieve whatever goal you're trying to achieve. A mentor is extremely valuable. And treat it that way. A mentor can save you from many mistakes and pitfalls from going in the wrong direction. Most times, a mentor has done what you're trying to do, so they should know where the mistakes are, the problems, where the challenges and difficulties are. The mentor will also have suggestions for how to get around or avoid these issues, if that's what you need. You can save a lot of time and money just by having a mentor.

Life Lesson Number 50:

Learn from Every Loss, Mistake, Failure, and Bad Decision

Even with this wonderful book of knowledge and wisdom and information, you're still going to make mistakes. You're still going to have failures, losses, and bad decisions, but when you do you have to try your best to learn from them. Revisit each one. Talk about it with yourself. Talk about it with your mentor. Just retrace those actions and those steps to reach your decisions. Analyse the whole situation, because the situation may come back and you will want to have learned from it and be able to have a better outcome the second time.

You don't want to keep making the same mistakes over and over again. You don't want to keep making the same bad decisions for the same situations. You want to take that information, analyse it, and use it again for your benefit. Not only that, you want it to be for someone else's benefit, like a friend, a business partner, a family member, whoever you know. People do not always learn from their own mistakes, failures, and whatnot, so one definite good way of just making yourself better is learning from yourself. Learn from the things you do well, and definitely learn from the things that did not go well. This can go a long way, and save you time, money, and stress.

Printed in Great Britain
by Amazon